Dear Atlas: I'm A Planet Still Orbiting Your

Supernova

This book is not a story about the ones we lose. It's a story about the people left behind.

# Letters

## Bargaining

Dear Atlas,

I'm having trouble beginning.

I'm trying. I swear.

That bouquet of flowers I bought for you today?

Okay, so I'm stalling.

This was a stupid idea.

## A(void)ance

The funeral was weird.

I keep replaying the moment in my head.

The reception went pretty smoothly.

You would've liked the music.

There was a small disturbance.

I couldn't stop thinking about all those graves.

It finally hit me.

I think I'm a masochist.

## Anger

Fuck off. Just...fuck off.

I'm still mad at you.

I don't want to remember you like that.

We were supposed to have more time.

## Depression

I'm sorry I didn't call.

Things are just really difficult right now?

I guess I know who my real friends are.

Brutus misses you.

Today would have been your 23rd birthday.

You're not the only person that lost someone.

I think I'm falling apart.

## Acceptance

I wish I knew.

Why I deleted your number.

I've been spending a lot of time at the hardware store lately.

I ride my bike a lot more now.

I don't know how to tell you this.

My Favourite Memory

Things You Did That Used to Annoy Me


## Healing.

I dreamed of you.

It Gets Easier.

You are not my whole day.

Thank You.

Do You Remember?

I'm thinking about mother's and daughters.

I met someone.

Aftermath

I can't believe it's been almost seven years.

# Bargaining

# Dear Atlas,

I talk to you a lot in my head. Does that make me crazy?
*Never crazy. Well, maybe a little mad but you know I don't mind.*

Anytime something happens, I go to tell you, and then I remember. I guess that's why I'm writing this. The sights, the sounds, the memories. They're all here for you. I just wish

*Wish what? You never finished your thought.*

It's funny what you think of in the aftermath. The first things that come back are never quite what you'd expect. There's this seismograph in the back of my head keeping track of all the ups and downs. The constant whirring is all about you.

I hate it. *That's not really fair. You're talking about me like I was a natural disaster. I never wanted to be something you survived...*

*I never asked for you to love me. It just happened.*

I'm having trouble beginning.

Well, beginning again.

It feels wrong to immortalize you in a love story. You were so much more than a love interest in the story of my life. But I wanted to put it down in words because *You're doing it again. You're losing the thread.*

All I have to remember you by are these fading vignettes, an odd collection of mementos, some photographs and this lump in my throat. *I'm sure with time the hurt will fade too. With time everything fades.*

The fact of the matter is memories fade, or they're wrong. Over time, everything fades. So, yeah. I'm afraid of forgetting. *Heh. We match ;)*

I'm afraid of forgetting the colour of your eyes in the afternoon sunlight or the sound of your laugh. It's getting harder and harder to recall the feel of your hand in mine.

*I never knew you'd miss those things this much.*

The way you looked sitting in my window seat, wearing one of my old t-shirts, your laptop balanced precariously on one knee—it's all seared into my memory. *Pervert. I love you too.*

But these moments—they're slipping through my fingers like tears, in the rain. I'm scared of what will happen when they're gone.

Really gone.
*But you don't need to be, love. That's just how things end.*

# I'm trying. I swear.

I just can't let you go yet. I keep finding memories of you in unsuspecting places. *You always did have a hard time letting go of things.*

A scratched-up CD in my dash console.
A hockey jersey shoved into a box we never unpacked.
A dumb joke on a birthday card.
Scuff marks left behind from when you rearranged the living room.

I remember the day I swore we'd rearrange things and make everything okay again. But I guess in the end we just moved furniture around.

*If we're being perfectly honest it was never about rearranging things at all. I just...needed some space.*

I still haven't figured out if you are a form of dark matter evident in the tiny fluctuations of our common space—or the gravity that shaped it. But, I'm glad that you're still here with me in a way. You've been shattered into so many pieces, and I'm still picking them up.

*NEW PICKUP LINE. You can pick me up anytime. ;)*

I know I should donate your things. But, once I find a memory of you, it demands another, and another, until I've amassed a collection. It's easy to keep falling in love with the memory of you. But, It's hard to let you go.

*Yeah. Memories are like that.*

The memories are dust particles shimmering in my atmosphere and glittering fragments embedded in the walls and the streets of the restaurants we loved. It all feels like you.

Still, it hurts. It's like trying to hold onto shards of glass. I just end up cutting myself on the edges. It all reminds me of you and it reminds me how much I miss you.

I promise I'll let go eventually. I just need a little more time.

It's okay to take your time. And, it's okay to not be okay.

# That bouquet of flowers I bought for you today?

They're your favourite. Daffodils.

I wish I could see your smile as you place them in some outrageously colourful tin can instead of watching them shiver in the autumn chill against your gravestone. *I can like things. :p*

And yet, the universe remains cruelly indifferent to what I want. At every turn, I am reminded that reality revolves around what is, and not, what it is as we would like it to be.

I've been ruminating on the concept of reincarnation. Specifically, the hallmarks of cosmic design. Or rather, the semblance of design. *Where are you going with this, love?*

In my life, the relationships I treasure most were formed in an atmosphere of strange coincidence and pervaded by a strong sense of deja vu. I have glimpsed a ghost in the faces of a thousand individuals.

The same spirit I found, complete, in you.

In the tangled weave of this universe, you were a red thread that had come loose. So, I tugged. And I marvelled in the thrill of watching you make my whole world come undone.

*You're losing the thread. Don't let it get away from you :)*

I can't help but feel that every familiar conversation, every choice made on instinct, all of it served to bring me closer to you. I want to believe that these moments of serendipity form a pattern that proves I was always destined to find you.

That, I was meant for you. *And, I was meant for you?*

The thought that we might meet again and again across a thousand lifetimes is a comforting one. Or at least it could be comforting if I didn't find the idea so hard to believe. You were always the spiritual one. Skepticism just seems to suit me better.

And that's okay. We might not have always been on the same page but we were usually reading the same chapter.

I feel like that's not a connection everybody gets to find in their lifetimes.

# Okay, so I'm stalling.

I'm spending so much time trying to capture the moments that succeeded it because it's too surreal right now. Too intimate. It hurts to look at it too long. *If it hurts, why are you doing this?*

This thing—I don't have the right words for it.

Will I ever have the right words?
*Does anybody?*

# This was a stupid idea.

How could I possibly begin to describe you? What combination of words could even come close to capturing my memories of you before they fade? *Stressy, depressy, aand sexy as hell?*

Some days you were bold and vibrant—sweeping everyone along like a wave. There was something about your smile that scattered the light in all directions.

You were brilliant. *Only took me a bajillion wires and dental appointments. :/*

Other days you were quiet, deeply troubled. Your brow would scrunch into this anxious furrow, and I could tell you had closed up on me. *It always surprised me that you could tell when I was sad. I've never had anybody really see me before.*

*Not like that anyway.*

There were days when your sharp wit became a vicious whip. A churning mess of anger and fear crashing against some invisible shoreline.

But you were my best friend. Whether you were rising or falling, I was there. Standing on the shoreline mesmerized by it all.

How could I not be?
*I love you too, dork.*

Part of me wants to preserve you as an ideal, a titan. I want to remember the Atlas that was both genius and muse, lover and beloved, teacher and student. I want to remember everything that made you so much larger than life.

But you would hate that. "A lie is a lie." you would declare, (usually with a hand gesture for emphasis).

To remember you just as you were, no more, no less. It's the only acceptable course of action and a difficult tightrope to walk. But I have to try.

So, where should I begin?

*Anywhere you want. <3 It's your story. Isn't it?*

# A(void)ance

# The funeral was weird.

It's very rare for all the members of a big family to be together in the same place at the same time. *Heh. Maybe not for mine.*

If you can get schedules to line up, you might get almost everyone together for Christmas or a family reunion. (Somebody always has to be late or get tied up with work at the last minute.)

*Let me guess, Uncle Mel, right?*

There's the timing to think about. Then you have to coordinate taking the kids out of school. There are commitments to think about. Promises to keep. Cars to pool.

But people always seem to find a way for the big three—weddings, births and funerals.

*You're forgetting Family Reunions.*

I guess it's because they're the only three events where the entire family dynamic can change. So, you need to be there. You need to witness it together. Or I guess bear witness to it?

I don't know. It's been a while since I've been to church. *I think it works. :)*

If I hadn't already, your funeral gave me the perfect opportunity to perfect the art of smiling and nodding when someone brings your name up in conversation.

---

*It's strange. Even if you're an absolute mess on the inside there's a switch that flips in social situations. You can hear your own voice laughing and smiling and you wonder if you were really sad at all.*

*It's like a polite stranger possesses your body to keep anybody from seeing you cry.*
At first, we milled about talking about this and that—avoiding the subject of the hour. Then the service began.

Poems were read, stories were told and people started crying.

From where I was sitting I could hear small packages of tissues being opened. Your grandmother, always ready with a pack of King mints, started passing them down the pews.
*Ah, yes. The Be Quiet Mints.*

It reminded me of the first time you took me to church.
*I distinctly remember you falling asleep.*

Listening to you try to explain what was happening during the service was both cute and silly. But, it made the whole thing worth it. You were so earnest. You really wanted me to be comfortable.

Probably because I'd never explained that I did grow up in a church. And, I chose to leave too.

*Wild. After three years you'd think it would have come up at least once.*

I wish you could've been there to explain it to me this time.

*What's there to explain? Here lies Atlas. Crushed by the weight of the world. Poetic isn't it?*

After the service, your sister began to pace back and forth with your crying nephew in her arms. I took him and tried to rock him for a bit. *He would have been about a year old then.*

Atlas, it's the strangest thing. He stared up at me with these big, dark eyes filled with tears, as if he knew you were gone. Maybe he did know, or maybe he was crying because everyone else was crying. Or maybe he was crying because he was hungry. *Pfft. You cry when you're hungry.*

I don't know. Babies are weird. *Pudgy little parasites.*

Occasionally, someone would come up to coo about how precious he was, but other than that, I didn't need to talk to anyone if I didn't feel like it. Still, plenty of people wanted to talk about you and I think I understand why.
*Funny, I always assumed there wouldn't be much to say.*
Somehow, hearing those stories, old and new, made it feel like you were still here.

So, seeking out family members, friends, and acquaintances in earnest felt like a way to legitimize that claim. The claim that until the last story is told and the memories have lapsed you are still living and breathing in our lives.

The stories help keep you alive a little.

At least, that's how it feels.

*Well, if it makes you happy I don't think it can be a bad thing?*

# I keep replaying the moment in my head.

Click. "Hello?"

It was your mother on the telephone. She'd been frantically messaging me for a couple of hours at this point asking if I could call her. I'd been asleep.

Sometimes, I wish I'd never picked up the phone. If I'd never picked up, I could stay in that moment before. That moment before I knew. That moment before her voice reached across the void and

With a few softly spoken words, she shattered the silence that had been there only moments before—that blissful, ignorant silence.

"Atlas and a friend were in an accident. They were driving late at night and crashed into a truck at a stoplight. They were brought into urgent care a couple of hours ago."

For a moment, I was relieved.

I was already planning what to bring you in the hospital. A silly 'Get Well Card,' some flowers and maybe a couple of books to read—something to make you smile while you were recovering.

"The other driver and the friend are recovering. Atlas is dead."

Dead.

The word hung in the air between us for what felt like an eternity. I never knew a word could feel so endless.

A few years ago, there was a fire—a neighbour's house. I woke up to the sounds of loud popping. Later I'd realize it was the groan of wood timbers buckling and cracking.

There was the frantic sound of a car alarm—then the sound distorting and falling silent.

From my window, I could see the glow. I swear I could feel the blistering heat on my hands and face from across the street.

I was mesmerized by the intensity. The inferno had engulfed the entire side of the house. Everything was smoke and ash and bright orange against the night sky, which somehow made the blackness seem darker.

Then firefighters arrived, bathing the entire scene in red and blue. I could see the jets of water being used to put out the flames from where I was standing.

So, I stood there at the window watching.

Within a few minutes, the fire had been put out and onlookers quickly dispersed, returning to their homes.

Thankfully, no one was hurt.

The fire had started in an attached garage, which was now completely gone, but the rest of the house had been spared. Mostly.

Still, the fire had consumed.

The garage was a heap of rubble collapsed inward. The neighbour's car sat in the middle of it all, warped and twisted with shattered glass all around. And for weeks, this putrid smell of burned wood and plastic remained.

For a little bit, the charred remains were a stark reminder of how unpredictable life can be. And yet, the thought that it could have been my house, and how much worse it could have been, faded quickly.

The skeletal remains became a part of the backdrop. And, eventually, I completely forgot about it.

It's funny how life gets away from you like that.

I don't even know when the garage was finally restored. I looked across the street one day, and the wreckage was gone. The house looked the same as any other house on our street. It was as if nothing had happened.

Dead is a house that's been burned down and rebuilt. Dead is a book you read so long ago you've forgotten that you even picked it up in the first place. Dead is gone. Gone and buried.

You know somewhere in the back of your mind what 'dead' means. Still, it doesn't feel real. Death.

People Die. Everybody dies. The people you love will die. One day, you will die too. It's a fact about life that you repeat until it becomes meaningless.

Dead...dead...dead.

And, now your mother was telling me you were dead? Just like that. Erased.

Everything after that moment felt surreal. Your mother kept talking, but her words were like rain falling on a tin roof. And I? I collected the runoff in a pill bottle I've been swallowing down every day since then.

Her every word fell with a sort of percussive quality, but the collection of words, together, became a deluge that was strangely heavy and muffled all at once.

"We are making funeral arrangements."

"We wanted you to hear it from us first."

"We'll let you know when we've figured things out."

It was all just noise. And I was drowning in it. How could you be gone? We just talked the other day about some things you'd left at my place.

"Please, let us know if you need anything."

And then she hung up. I can still hear the click.

Atlas. Dead.

# The reception went pretty smoothly.

The funeral staff had prepared a small private area for close friends and family to sit and eat.

Mostly, people talked and walked around and ate. They visited for a while, sniffling and hugging. There were small outbursts of laughter and muffled cries.

Your sister passed out styrofoam cups of coffee and orange slices. The little ones would look around cautiously before stuffing their faces full of Timbits. Of course, their parents noticed, but we were all glad to see the kids acting like kids.

I think there's this deep fear that grief and loss can do something irreparable to young people. I mean, look at what it does to adults.

So, nobody said anything. But, the kids seemed pleased they had gotten away with this small act of mischief.

Mostly, I watched. I didn't feel like talking.

As I ate silently I thought about the funeral staff. They never lost their composure. I couldn't imagine being around grieving families all day every day. It hurts enough seeing yours this undone.

Then I thought about your brother. Maybe having a function to serve helped him walk straight that day. Did you know he officiated for you?

The night before, he went to bed with puffy eyes and the smell of cannabis clinging to him. But, he was a pillar of strength the day of your funeral.

You would have been so proud of him.

# You would've liked the music.

The funeral ruined your favourite songs for me. Now every time I listen to them I choke. Still, I think you would've liked the songs everyone picked.

Boxes by the Goo Goo Dolls was a popular choice. It's also one of the hardest songs to avoid.

I hear it when I switch through radio stations. In fucking car commercials. It's everywhere.

That Billy Joel song you love.

One of your nieces picked Counting Houses by Luz? She said you played that song for her when you drove to the mall together.

Honestly, you were an awful singer. But when I listen to those songs I can almost hear your voice. It's a good kind of hurt? I think.

But the song that kills me the most is Fool For Waiting. Dan Mangan. Every time I hear it I can feel the tears well up.

After all, it was our song.

# There was a small disturbance.

During the night a few of us were awoken by the sound of your brother and some of your friends drunkenly singing and stumbling about in the hallways. Apparently, there was a bar within walking distance from the hotel we were staying at.

I was still awake so I didn't really mind. And I feel like you would've been out there in the hallway with them anyways. You never liked all the crying at funerals. Still, it was pretty late.

Others quieted them because they'd wake the children who had just fallen asleep.

Later that night your brother and I got to talking. Mostly, we talked about you. I'd never been that close with him. All I knew is that you loved him and things hadn't exactly been easy between the two of you.

He'd always been kind of a black sheep. And you were always sort of grey.

Your brother wears his pain naked. He always has. All those worn-down gears, stretched springs, and interlocking bits of wire. Visible.

The hinges that creak and pop in places. The pendulum. The broken ticker. Audible.

But for a moment the pain I read in his eyes was so private I felt like I was intruding. And it makes me wonder how long a body can sustain itself before it finally falls to pieces.

*Your clock is wound. All the time we have is now.*

# I couldn't stop thinking about all those graves.

I don't know who died or who put them there. But there are so many people buried next to you. So many names.

Honestly, they just look like cut stones with names and numbers on them. It's really weird that I'm supposed to stand here and feel something. It's morning and the weather's cool—overcast.

This place doesn't feel like you. It feels like nothing.

Every time someone dies it makes me think about my own life. And standing here thinking about you I can't help but notice the graves that have completely worn away.

There's no one left to remember them.

We can pickle it and paint it, fixed and pretty, but it is still death. Under all this dirt, there are bodies and caskets that have completely decomposed. And there are people here who are only names and numbers now.

What happens when there's no one left to remember you? Is that the last step? Is that when you're really dead and gone?

Maybe that's why we try so hard for our fifteen minutes of fame. Those extra precious seconds where people remember that we existed keep us alive that little bit longer.

Until, ashes to ashes, and the rest is rust and stardust.

I still don't know how to find the words to describe you. Am I failing you? Once I'm gone, and there's no one left to remember you, do you die a second time?
It feels fake trying to express it in a eulogy. Contrived. Inadequate. I did try to write you one. I tried. But I couldn't bring myself to read it.

I couldn't do it. Because then, it would be real. And, I wasn't ready for it to be real yet. I'm still not ready.

I guess this is an apology for that.

## It finally hit me.

I am haunted by the space you've left behind. I didn't feel it right away—that emptiness you'd been occupying. But when I felt it, it hit me like a ton of bricks.

I keep choking on the lump in my throat. Can you die from a broken heart? Because it hurts. A lot. I think I've finally cried enough for the tears to stop and ended up seeking refuge in bed. I guess that's a good thing right?

It's warm and safe and lonely. I keep counting to ten, telling myself I'll get up. But, it's been three days and I'm still here.

I don't know if it's worse or better, knowing nobody will miss me for a while. I slept so much but I still feel so tired. Maybe if I close my eyes I can stay in this warm, cosy headspace.

Maybe if I'm lucky, I won't wake up. I don't have the energy. I just want to sleep.

I remember staying up the night before the funeral. I had the hotel room to myself. I spent the night scrolling through Facebook. Reading through memorial posts and old pictures of you. It was then that I first began to realize just how much of you I never got to meet.

The first time I cried it was for your mother. I couldn't cry then for myself. It didn't feel real yet. It still doesn't.

She's always been so strong, so disciplined and restrained. Cold. But the heartbreak in her voice after that phone call was so raw and vulnerable it hurt.

Some nights, you'd stay up crying, racked with despair. Certain that there was nothing you could ever do that would be good enough for her. Some nights you'd sit and stare into nothing, wondering if she ever even loved you.

I wish you could have heard the confirmation that those fears were wrong. No matter how many nights I held you, rocked you, swore to you that you were enough, there was a part of you that couldn't believe me.

I'll be perfectly honest, when I broke I ugly cried. A lot. Loud sobs followed by uneven gasps for air. There's this tightness in my chest. It's like I can't stop. I'm not even thinking about anything specific when it happens.

Almost like the aftershock. Is loss a kind of trauma? Does it seep into your muscles and tissue?

Even now that I'm calm my eyes are burning. When I close them I can feel the tears well up again. Every time I blink.

In the room next to mine a couple was making love. Hotel walls are thin.

The sound of their passionate embrace conjured up the phantom memory of your arms thrown around my neck— wonderfully long legs wrapped around my waist. We were like that once. Young and stupid.

I can remember burying my face in your neck to hide a smile and the pull of your fingers tangled in my hair. Recklessly vulnerable. But together. Invincible.

And, in the early morning, with the sun filtering in through the curtains, we wound up curled around each other like quotation marks. Never to be separated.

In those peaceful moments between 'yesterday' and 'today' nothing else mattered but you and me. How could it? How could anything ever compare to the feeling of holding the whole universe in my arms?

# I think I'm a masochist.

I've been scrolling through Facebook, reading and re-reading the memorial posts. Looking through old pictures of you, smiling and happy. Sometimes I put on old videos of you. But it hurts hearing your voice.

I stopped crying at some point. So, that's good. I think.

Sometimes, I don't think about you at all. I disappear into a game or a book or my work and thoughts of you disappear too. But, it doesn't last.

If I pause for too long, I remember.

So, sometimes it feels better to sit with it. Sometimes, it feels better to hurt.

# Anger

# Fuck off. Just...fuck off.

I left something out on purpose when I was telling you about the funeral and it hasn't been sitting right with me.

I don't know what's worse. That when you die the people who have picked away at you come out of the woodwork to shed crocodile tears—or that some of them don't have the decency to shut up.

Your Aunt and her brood came to the funeral. I can't imagine why.

She spent most of the service dragging her sheepish looking children around from person to person—dabbing at fake tears with a balled up kleenex.

One of those black pillbox hats fastened precariously to one side in such a way she needed to keep reaching up to check that it was still firmly in place.

I tried to avoid her as best I could. From the way she kept checking her phone, I knew the funeral couldn't end soon enough for her.

All day I'd been overhearing her clucking sympathetically "I warned Atlas if they kept up with all that drinking and smoking it'd kill them. Didn't I say that?"

"Oh, I know just how you feel! Our little terrier, Bella passed away this summer. Heart failure. The kids are absolutely devastated."

But, then my luck ran out.

I felt a tap on the shoulder and turned around only to find myself staring right into her oversized sunglassess. So, I put on a pained smile and and greeted her through gritted teeth.

"Jen. So good to see you."

I answered most of her questions on autopilot.
'So, how are you holding up?'
'Awful isn't it?'
'Together for four years, right?'

But, just as escape was in reach, one sentence fell from her lips and stirred up something inside my chest.

'I told Atlas they needed to go on a diet...excersise more. Stop drinking. Get help for those anger issues.'

'Maybe if she'd have listened this wouldn't have happened. God only gives us what he knows we can handle.'

I was so angry I couldn't breathe.

# I'm still mad at you.

I didn't even get to say goodbye. Not really.

The whole thing makes me wonder if it was worth it. Was it
worth it for us to be happy for a little bit, even though it
ended up sad? Or would it have been better if the whole thing
never happened?

Why'd you have to leave when I needed you to stay?

You could've stayed the night. Gotten a hotel or called someone to come pick you up. But you decided to drive home instead. Just this once, you could have decided not to be stubborn.

I loved that about. But just this once, you could've made a different choice. What the fuck were you even doing driving around at one in the morning?

Maybe not directly but, you chose. You didn't know it then, but you chose how you would die. And that choice you made put you at an intersection with a red light and a semi-truck on an icy road.

The very definition of the wrong place at the wrong time.

And, I know it's not really anybody's fault. But I wish it was. I wish there was an answer. I wish there was someone to blame.

I guess it's kind of ironic that I'm standing here, an atheist, searching the heavens for an answer to a simple question— why. When all I'll ever get is silence.

Wanna know the worst part?

I don't think there's an explanation that could ever make this feel okay.

There is no one to blame. Not even you. It just happened. One day you were here, and then one day, you were gone.

So, why am I still so angry? And what the fuck am I supposed to do about it if there's nothing to be angry at?

How do I stand here and just accept that for us, the stars refused to shine?

I don't want to remember you like that.

There's something very intimate about watching a person be themself. It's so sad that when you see someone as they really are it ruins them.

I don't know when it started but, little by little we changed. Somewhere between here and now, we didn't just grow apart.

We grew up.

We tried to fix it. But there's only so much duct

tape in the world that you can use to try to build a bridge across a canyon. Eventually, the whole thing will collapse in on itself.

When you told me how you felt, we both cried like babies and I held you for a long time. But not long enough. I thought the end of us was the end of the world and I didn't want to let you go.

I guess fate had a cruel way of making sure I had to learn, eh?

The first time I lost you I thought my heart was broken. But it kept on beating just the same. The second time I felt like I had died. Still, my heart kept beating. It just hurt more.

We hadn't even told your family yet. I still don't know if I should or not.

Still, I looked and looked at you that day and every day after. And every time I looked, I knew just as clearly that I loved you.

But right before the moment I lost you, I forgot that fact. Together became a sudden strangeness. And, I'm going to keep hating myself for that for a long time.

We were supposed to have more time.

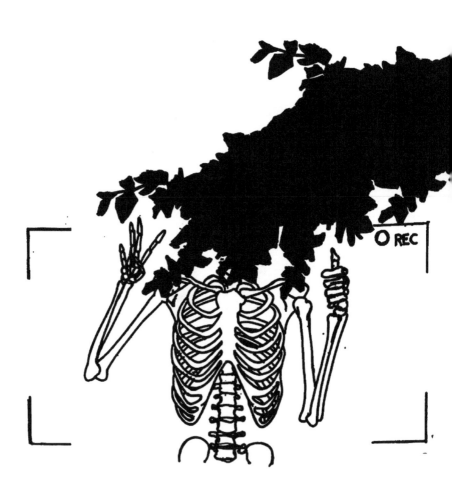

I could've called you more or done a better job remembering your birthdays, splurged a bit more on presents. There just never seemed to be enough time.

You always took the worst pictures of me and then you'd laugh.

I've always hated the way I look in photographs. You would insist that I looked beautiful and it'd make me blush. In a good way.

Now, I can't look at old photos of you without crying. I wish I'd taken more when we had the chance.

The main thing I think about is how stupid it is that I didn't realize it sooner. I wasted so many years being miserable because I assumed we'd have more time. I don't want to do that anymore.

I keep counting the one mores; the kisses, the hugs, the meals, the Netflix binges. And it all adds up to not enough.

Not enough time before we get to the part where I have to say goodbye.

I'd always assumed we'd have more time. More time to travel and see the world. More time to talk about having kids. There was supposed to be more time.

We never got to buy that stupid cat. I kept fighting you on it but, honestly, I know you would've changed my mind eventually. And, we were going to save up enough to get that three bedroom townhouse with the porch swing. Just like you always wanted.

And, I swear if you were still here we would've. If I knew this was how it was going to end we would've done it all sooner. All of it.

The backpacking trip, the murder mystery dinner, dance lessons. All of it. We were going to, I swear. But, I kept pushing it back.

And, now it's too late. I thought we'd have five, ten, fifteen years but we only got three. You're gone and I'm here. And, that feels really unfair.

# Depression

# I'm sorry I didn't call.

I'm a coward. I know eventually, I'm going to need to pick up the phone and call. Just, not tonight.

I can't. I can't do the niceties and the condolences. I just want to feel normal.

# Things are just really difficult right now?

Everything is beginning to pile up. Without you, everything is a mess. I can't seem to find the energy to load the dishwasher. We've run out of spoons. And, I lost the stupid TV remote.

I'm muddling through the day. Mostly.

I try to keep myself busy. Sometimes I'll turn on the radio or my computer and listen to videos. It's background noise—something to drown out the silence. I'm functioning. Robotically, but I am surviving.

Surviving. It makes it sound like you were a hurricane or a tornado that swept through the area upending everything I've ever known. A tempest.

It's hard to throw myself into my work. My head is all cluttered. Noisey. I feel like a browser with too many tabs open.

# I guess I know who my real friends are.

It's funny. One day you wake up and all your friends are gone. And maybe, part of that's your fault. It gets really hard for people to be upset or happy around you in a regular way when you're grieving.

You sink. You sink into this pit. And sometimes you're so busy frantically thrashing around you don't even notice when people are trying to throw you a lifeline. Instead, you end up trying to pull them down with you.

After you died I thought people became different. But maybe I became different. I started pushing them away. Little by little.

Because, celebrating these moments without you, feels like I'm accepting moving forward without you. It feels like a betrayal.

You aren't here. And I can't help feeling a little left behind. While we all move forward in this exhausting world you're not here. Sometimes I envy you.

It's easier to live in your shadow than to walk in your footsteps. Cold but still easier.

## Brutus misses you.

Maybe, even more than me. Is that possible for a dog?

Remember that time Brutus got out of the house and took off running? We must've walked up and down every back alley in the neighbourhood calling his name. All the while you were making jokes, trying to keep the mood light.

When we finally found him he was darting back and forth across someone's lawn. Completely oblivious to the panic he'd caused and the garden bed he'd destroyed.

Mostly, he sits and whines at me with this pitying look in his big brown eyes until I get up to feed him in the morning. And then again when I get home.

We walk around the block once or twice and nap on the couch for a bit. Pretty much his whole day.

Sometimes, when he slumps down onto his dog bed and his eyes flicker to the door I know he's waiting for you to open it. Sometimes, I'm waiting too.

# Today would have been your 23rd birthday.

The ice cream cake. The candles.

The brilliant smile on your face that would have put the whole scene to shame.

It's a photograph framed only in my memory.

Another one I'll never have with you.

# You're not the only person that lost someone.

I can't get those words out of my head. Atlas, I messed up. Royally.

I yelled at your sister the other day for inviting herself over. In these moments when all I can do is think of you, interruptions fill me with unspeakable anger and shame. I felt this surge of anger rise up in me. So, I chewed her out.

I tried to take it back.

'I'm sorry. I'm terrified. Atlas and I moved in together right out of college. I've never been alone. Until now. I just need some space.'

'You must be tired.' She said softly. 'You're not alone. You're not. I promise. We're all here for you.'

But I couldn't focus on her words. Instead, I just got angrier. How could she possibly understand? I didn't have to say it either, I swear she could hear it in my voice.

And for the first time, I saw your sister. The perfectly composed exterior cracked, just a little bit.

'You're not the only person who lost someone.'

And then it clicked.

The parade of casseroles, organizing visits, the rigid adherence to business as usual. I've been so wrapped up in my own grief I didn't think. Your sister has been watching your family fall apart without you. And I haven't been helping.

She's been here the whole time, sitting and listening to everyone talk about you. But, I don't think any of us really thought that maybe she needed to talk about you too.

I didn't think. Atlas, she looks so much like you when she cries. Those big dark eyes. There was a piece of you right in front of me and I forgot.

'We all miss Atlas.' And then she left. We haven't talked since.

# I think I'm falling apart.

I didn't feel like eating. I haven't in a while. So, when Christmas rolled around I just drank. A lot. After a while everything just started to blur together. And I couldn't escape this crushing feeling of guilt and self-hatred.

Is this what you felt like when you were alive? Is this why you started shutting me out? I think I finally understand what it means to collapse inward. I think I finally understand you.

It's lonely. Really lonely.

Atlas, I can't breathe. I'm

Suffocating.

# Acceptance

# I wish I knew.

The story of your life and all the thoughts that kept you up at night. Sometimes I'd wake up in the dark and reach out my hand, searching for your warmth in the space you'd left behind.

Then, I'd close my eyes and listen to the clinking of a spoon against your teacup.

I used to wonder. Why didn't you wake me? If it was a bad dream or an anxious thought, keeping you up at night, I'd have listened. I'd have held you in my arms.

I'd have told you it was going to be okay as many times as it'd take for you to believe me.

But over time, I became used to those moments of unknowability. As the years passed, we grew together, but there would always be a part of you apart from me.

You carried the weight of the world on your shoulders with a smile and a shrug. And we were comfortable that way.

Now, as I lie awake, keenly aware of the emptiness you've left behind, I close my eyes, and all I hear is silence.

# Why I deleted your number.

You want to know what the last thing I ever sent you was?

| |
|---|
| **Sat, Sept 9,** 2:35 AM |
| Are you still up? |
| **Mon, Sept 10,** 2:30 PM |

Sorry I haven't been answering. Just have a lot going on right now.

No problem

**Wed, Sept 11,** 1:30 AM

Are we still friends?

Of course we're still friends.

You promise?

I promise

Mkaay but do you super promise?

Atlas

I super duper promise

Dork

Hehe okay

**Fri, Sept 13,** 7:30 PM

There's something to be said about being able to document these small moments in such a concrete way. I always hated it before. The constant chatter of updates and notifications, read message bubbles. I didn't want to live my life through a screen.

I just wanted something real. And, you were that real thing.

I don't know if you ever saw my last text. We had slowly begun to figure things out. This being 'on break' thing. But it still hurt. So, I didn't respond right away. And I hate myself for it.

I thought that if I waited maybe it wouldn't really be over. That maybe you'd come to your senses. And this overlong, miserable summer, would end. I took you for granted.

I don't even care now. Friends, lovers, acquaintances. I just want you back in my life. But, it's too late now.

I didn't have the heart to delete your contact info for almost two years. I found myself holding my phone like it was you. Just seeing your name, knowing that I could reread our old messages made me feel like maybe I could still text you.

But I can't.

I can't keep obsessing over the way we left things between us.

I can't keep reminding myself of what I could or should have said.

I can't keep kicking myself for losing what we had—one second too late to fix a damn thing.

I miss you too much.

# I've been spending a lot of time at the hardware store lately.

The faucet is leaking. Some of the doors have squeaky hinges. And the closet door fell off its track a couple days ago. It's taken a lot of WD-40, (and a few too many Youtube videos), but I'm getting pretty good at fixing things.

I'm trying to keep myself busy, you know?

Some days it feels like I'm not progressing at all, other days I think 'maybe a little'. And, that's good. I want to get better.

I learned how to bake a cheesecake the other day. It actually turned out pretty well. You would've loved it.

I'm sorry. I can't.

I'm trying to be positive for you but I can't. I'm sorry. I'm so sorry. I'm trying really hard to feel normal again. But I can't.

Atlas, I'm scared I can't do this without you.

I feel like I don't have control over anything anymore. The place is a mess and everytime I fix one problem, another one pops up. Everything is piling up. I'm suffocating.

I can't be with people. And I can't be alone.

If I stop for too long I can feel the grief clawing at my throat. So, I keep my hands busy and I fill the deafening silence with white noise.

I used to leave work early so we could have dinner together. Now I go home as late as possible and spend my free time binging sitcoms.

I find it reassuring that no matter what happens, at the end of 30 minutes everything will be okay again. They're just shows about good, likeable people who love each other. And, right now I really need that.

I'm just hoping that if I keep myself distracted, one day my fragile heart will stop; stop jolting at the sound of a phone notification or shuffling at the front door because I know. I know that it will never be you.

Because, you're never coming back.

# I ride my bike a lot more now.

It's been two years now. But, from time to time bad weather awakens my fears. One late night on a bad road and it could've been my mom putting my dad in the ground, or me or my brother.

I've been seeing a therapist. Not just because of you. For everything. I've been having these attacks?

It starts with this ringing in my ears. Then everything begins to go black. Like a curtain or a thick dark cloud descending around my head. Everything is both muffled and so painfully loud. Everything is too bright and too dark all at once.

There's this painful pit in my stomach. Like butterflies but worse. Like all the muscles in my stomach are seizuring. And my chest begins to hurt.

It feels like dying.

# I don't know how to tell you this.

I was up again with Brutus last night. I don't think it'll be long now. His breathing comes in short wheezes. But he still wags his tail playfully when I pet him. I couldn't help it. I wished that he would just die already. I couldn't bear to hear him suffering.

Each breath sounds so heavy and laborious.

After your things were divided up by your mother and sorted I ended up coming home with a Rubbermaid bin full of stuff I'd given you. But I haven't gotten the chance to open it and go through everything until now.

Every time I tried Brutus would begin to cry and pace back and forth. He misses you a lot. And I don't know if there's a way to explain that you won't be coming back to visit. I wish there was.

Sometimes it made me angry.

I just wanted to get things sorted. Maybe, I wished a little too hard.

But, as much as it hurts at least it feels like there's a reason for me to cling to. With you, we never got to see the end coming.

You were here, it was brilliant.

And now you're gone.

Soon, it'll be 'et tu Brute?'. I don't know how much more I can take.

# My Favourite Memory

Our first date was a disaster! I'm honestly baffled that I
even got a second date. And yet, by some stroke of luck, you
thought my socially awkward, dorky-looking self was 'sweet'
and 'cute'. You didn't even mind that I forgot my wallet and
you had to pay for lunch. What a weirdo.

Despite your lack of taste, I was determined to make date
number two memorable because I just knew. I knew you were
something special.

In my head I had it all planned out. I'd pick you up in my car—you'd look amazing just like you always do. We'd stop for pizza on the way up to my favourite spot to go stargazing. I'd glance over and notice you shivering.

And there—overlooking the river with the stars above us—I'd lean in, cup your face in my hands and kiss you just like I'd been imagining every day since we met.

When we got out of the car, you slipped your hand into mine and it just...felt *right.*

We got to the spot and set down blankets and pillows, pulled out snacks and drinks—I even managed to get my hands on a portable speaker so we could listen to music. For a while, we just talked. I almost forgot about the stars.

It took a few tries, but you were finally able to make out the summer triangle. And, that's when I told you the story.

It's always been one of my favorites.

One Autumn day, Vega, the seventh daughter of the Jade emperor—ruler of the celestial court—descended from the heavens to bathe in a lotus garden where she was seen by Altair, a poor cowherd.

They fell in love and eventually married. Finding their rhythm easily—her at her loom, him tending to the fields and his flock. A simple life but a happy one. They even had children together.

However, the Jade Emperor was disgusted by their daughter's lowly marriage and, enraged, ordered she be whisked back up to heaven. When the soldiers came to carry her away the lovers cried and plead but nothing could be done.

Their love was forbidden.

In every version of the story, Altair gets help from one of his ox to reach the heavens, (who just so happens to be a former celestial). In some versions, Altair himself was once a celestial who fell in love with Vega and was banished to earth with no memories, only for the two to find each other again.

Whatever the version, the lovers refused to let anything separate them. So, when Altair gathers up their two children and pursues her across the heavens their reunion seems inevitable. Until, just as the family is about to be reunited the Jade emperor creates an immense, impassable river between them—the milky way.

And the lovers stand there gazing across the vast distance, heartbroken.

I paused for a moment then, embarrassed by the intensity in your eyes. I had never seen you so enthralled by anything. I could feel my heart pounding and hoped you couldn't hear it.

Just when it seemed all hope was lost thousands of magpies took pity on the couple and formed a bridge across the river.

When the family ran across the bridge and embraced, in tears, the Jade emperor took pity on them.

Now, the lovers stand at the edge of the river every day, waiting for the one day each year when the Jade emperor creates a bridge, allowing their little family to be made whole.

When I finished the story you gave me this big mischievous grin and I swear my heart stopped dead. It was like I blinked and suddenly your face was inches away from mine.

When you kissed me all I could muster was a 'thank you'. Like an idiot. And then we were kissing again.

I'd always harboured a little bit of hope that we were made to defy gravity but with you, right then, I felt like I was already flying.

It wasn't how I planned our first kiss to go. But, it was still perfect somehow. It felt like the stars were aligning for just us two.

When we finally came up for air you kissed my forehead and said in a soft voice I felt deep in my core 'it's cute when you get all nerdy and shy on me'.

And in that moment I loved you completely.

Of course, it took you a little bit longer for you. But when it happened...all at once we were clumsily, shamelessly, stupidly, in love.

I never realized the ocean is full of stars.

## Things You Did That Used to Annoy Me

Laughing, crying, talking, fighting, kissing, eating. All these small acts that bind us together play like a short film.

But it's the absence of certain things that take up the most space somehow.

The countertops stay clean for days. There are no spills or kitchen utensils strewn haphazardly about from one of your latest experiments.

The dishes get rinsed, washed and put away neatly in the cupboard after every meal.

There is no one to ask me what kind of shampoo I think I would like or if I want to try a new kind of toothpaste this week.
And definitely, no one to buy me those things after I've already said I am perfectly fine with my 2-in-1 and that I haven't really thought about my toothpaste that much.

When I get home from a long day at work there's nobody to fuss over how much water I've had to drink or if I'd like to order pizza as a treat when I'm really not that hungry.

My life is simpler now. Quiet. Strange.

There are so many things that you touched and when your hands came away, they became more like you. To the point that you are even in the absence of things.

You are here and not here. In the nothing and the everything. Both alive and dead.

A paradox of quantum superposition.

# Healing

## I dreamed of you.

I woke up from a strange dream. We were sitting in the
living room, and everyone was excitedly talking to you. I

knew I had so much to say, but I also knew when I woke up, you'd be gone.

You looked at me and told me not to worry. I could visit you in my dreams whenever I wanted. I knew it was a lie, and I know it is now. But I wanted to believe it so badly.

I wanted to believe that it was really you—talking and laughing, making silly jokes. But I can't. I won't.

Still, in that moment, I felt at peace. Whatever tightness had been compressing my chest loosened a bit. It felt good. It felt good to think for a moment that you hadn't really left.

Everything moves on, doesn't it?

## It Gets Easier.

Every day; pushing this boulder uphill gets easier. But you have to do it every day. That's the hard part.

It doesn't really feel like progress, putting in all that work just to watch it roll back down again—over and over. But you have to try.

All you can do is try.

And, I suppose it depends on the kind of progress you're trying to make. No matter what you do, the boulder's displacement will remain the same, zero.

But, if you keep pushing that boulder uphill every day, the distance you've walked will climb. On a good day, that fact can feel like progress.

At least, that's what I'm choosing to believe.

# You are not my whole day.

Sometimes I don't think about you at all. But when I do think of you, I feel guilty for forgetting.

It comes upon me suddenly. I'll see a social media post or remember a gift you gave me, look at the odd number of Christmas stockings on the mantle and remember the space you used to occupy is still there.

And suddenly, I am grieving again.

Sometimes, I feel guilty for living. I feel guilty for being happy because you're not here.

Thank You.

The facts are that stars die. The night sky is full of dead stars. But from here, they don't look doomed—From here, they shine. Sometimes, I find that thought haunting.

Perhaps all this time, I've been alone. But no. I'm not alone because of you.

When we met, I got to see emergent properties in action. Before you, I was limited in a way I couldn't yet recognize. I was aware of pain and myself. A collection of hydrogen atoms. Singular.

And then there was you. A breath of fresh air I didn't know my lungs needed. And suddenly, I was conscious of you—of us.

Together, we formed something more complex. Plurality. And from that emerged something precious.

Together we evolved. Like hydrogen and oxygen we became water. New properties emerged. We became more than the sum of our parts.

I am grateful for the privilege of loving you once. Because before you, I never knew I could love someone so much. Sometimes, loving you hurt. A lot. Losing you still hurts every day.

But I can't undo the chemical change that being loved by you put in motion. And, honestly I wouldn't want to.

Our moments fall around us like rain. Impactful but temporary. Still, if I close my eyes, I can see your light. It seems to carry on ahead.

# Do You Remember?

There's something special that happens when two celestial bodies orbit each other—gravitational waves.

The waves spread out like a ripple in a pond, stretching and compressing space-time and everything in it as they pass.

From where I'm standing now, I can still hear the faint echo of the first time we collided.

I'd have given anything to know what was going through your mind. We'd chat in between classes, sometimes during class.

We liked a lot of the same things. But I could never figure out how you felt about me—until that rainy summer day when you padlocked your bike to mine. So, I sat outside on the campus lawn, waiting. I was so crazy about you I didn't even mind that the grass was wet.

When you finally did show up, you caught me by surprise. "I was just wondering if you were ever going to ask me out?"

For a second, I was speechless. Was it that obvious? But, I think mostly I was in shock because I'd been imagining this moment all semester.

I think I managed to spit out "Do you want to-" before you cut me off with "Yes."

I was so happy and anxious and giddy that I started laughing, and then you started laughing.

I loved your laugh. I swear, it was the greatest sound in the world.

I can't think of a specific moment, or a look or a word that made me yours. It was a collection of things that hit at just the right frequency to create the kind of mechanical resonance that collapses bridges.

But even those waves reverberating through me are not the strongest ones I've ever felt.

Unfortunately, the most powerful gravitational waves are usually the product of violent events—cosmic shipwrecks and exploding stars.

Sure, like any wave, the ripples diminish in size the further away you get from the crash. But I feel like I'm standing in the wake of a supernova.

Gravity tried to squeeze you into nothingness, and for a while, your nuclear core burned bright and hot enough to hold out. Until it didn't.

One day gravity won, and you collapsed inward.

And the resulting explosion was so bright and so overwhelming, for a long time after, I couldn't see the stars.

That day, you were here with your beautiful smile and your laugh. And then, you were gone forever.

## I'm thinking about mother's and daughters.

I'm thinking about how parents bring children into the world. They raise their kids, knowing one day they'll have to leave them behind.

It must be hard to make room.

Make room. Is that how you make losing life easier to understand—new life? You might get six or seven years or twenty two or three as a reward for bearing them. But sometimes you end up burying them instead.

I've been thinking a lot.
About you, about me and sometimes
about Annabelle Lee.

Hear me out.

Poe says it was the wind that chilled her and the angels that killed her. He insists it's the heavens that wanted to tear those two lovers apart. But it wasn't. It was Poe.

In the end, it was Poe that shut her up in that sepulchre by the sounding sea. It's always the poets, the writers and the artists that kill the muse. They perpetuate tragedy in the name of art.

But I can't say for certain if the beauty makes it hurt any less. It all feels so senselessly, needlessly cruel.

# I met someone.

I think you'd like them. I've been meaning to tell you—I just didn't know how. I know. I'm being foolish. You've always said that you would never want to stand in the way of my happiness.

I think the first time you said that to me it was when we decided to take a break. Looking back I know we had our problems but they all seem so small now.

I-I don't understand it myself. Lying awake listening to the sound of your breathing, just holding you in my arms—my heart always felt so full.

I couldn't even imagine having enough room left over for anyone else. And after you I honestly didn't know if I would ever feel that happy again.

But, for the first time in a long time I think it's possible.

I'm scared of course. Scared that maybe if I mess up there won't be a next time. Scared that no matter how hard I try I'll keep thinking of you, comparing them to you. I don't want to replace you. Ever.

All I know is that I've been stuck.

After the crash you were gone and all I knew was silence. So, I told myself to just keep moving forward. I was a celestial body orbiting the scattered remains of a dead star. Somehow, the phantom pull of your gravity kept me on a course we once chartered together.

But, I think I'm finally beginning to understand what a life without you could look like. I want to try at least. Really try.

I'm trying to look at it like a new chapter or a new star. I might be orbiting a different one now, but it will never diminish the light and warmth I found in you.

So, this isn't goodbye. This is I love you. I always will. It's 'I'll talk to you later'.

After all, nothing's as good if you don't share it.

# Aftermath

/ˈaftərˌmaTH/

I think it's time to drop your things off at the donation center.

I thought that grief was a mourning period. A length of time that ends. But I'm beginning to realize there is no coming out the other side. There is only the choice to keep living in the aftermath.

There is only the choice to keep letting go.
To keep saying goodbye and thank you,
for the memories.

Little by little I am learning. Things will always feel different without you. But, I will be okay. It's okay to feel alive. It's okay to be happy. It's okay for life to be beautiful again.

It will all just be slightly different now.
For better or for worse I'm different now too.

Don't get me wrong.

Knowing how it'd all play out between us, (and even how it'd end), I'd fall in love with you all over again. Because even in the aftermath, I am better for having known you. What we had was perfect for us then.

I only wish you could see me now.

# I can't believe it's been almost seven years.

I'm still figuring out how to keep living without you. It gets a little better every day but it's still hard sometimes.

I don't know why life is like this. I wish I knew. I just don't.

But I do know that there's a six decimal point range where life as we know it can exist by accident. And the chances of you, just as you are, in the place, in the time and the space that you occupy are infinitesimally improbable.

The chances of us meeting, are even smaller.

But here you are. Raging against the universe for one brief, blink-and-you'll-miss-it, second—a tiny dot, on an endless timeline. So, powerfully, wonderfully, vibrantly alive.

By definition a miracle.

And I think this precious incarnation, this mathematical divinity, was worth every second of heartbreak.

**Dear Atlas**

978-1-7782795-1-5 (ebook)
978-1-7782795-0-8 (paperback)

10 9 8 7 6 5 4 3 2 1
Published in Canada

Manufactured by Amazon.ca
Bolton, ON

28500082R00070